LIGHT SHINING
IN BUCKINGHAMSHIRE

LIGHT SHINING IN BUCKINGHAMSHIRE

Caryl Churchill

THEATRE COMMUNICATIONS GROUP
NEW YORK
2018

Light Shining in Buckinghamshire is published by Theatre Communications Group, Inc., 520 Eighth Avenue, 24th Floor, New York, NY 10018-4156.

This volume is published in arrangement with Nick Hern Books Limited, The Glasshouse, 49a Goldhawk Road, London, W12 8QP.

This publication is made possible in part by the New York State Council on the Arts with the support of Governor Andrew Cuomo and the New York State Legislature.

TCG books are exclusively distributed to the book trade by Consortium Book Sales and Distribution.

A catalog record for this book is available from the Library of Congress.

ISBN 978-1-55936-595-6 (paperback)

Cover art: Photograph by Sorted, Banner by Ed Hall

Cover design by Lisa Govan

First TCG Edition, December 1996

New Edition, April 2018

Light Shining in Buckinghamshire was revived in the Lyttelton auditorium at the National Theatre, London, on 15 April 2015, with the following cast:

COBBE, *a gentleman*	Joshua James
VICAR	Daniel Flynn
JP 1	Jonathan Dryden Taylor
JP 2	Simon Manyonda
MARGARET BROTHERTON, *a vagrant*	Ashley McGuire
STAR, *a corn merchant*	Nicholas Gleaves
BRIGGS, *a working man*	Trystan Gravelle
FRIEND, *a working man*	Leo Bill
MAN, *a vagrant*	Alan Williams
PREACHER	Sargon Yelda
HOSKINS, *a vagrant preacher*	Adelle Leonce
CLAXTON, *a working man*	Joe Caffrey
CLAXTON'S WIFE	Amanda Lawrence
WOMAN WITH MIRROR	Elizabeth Chan
HER FRIEND	Ann Ogbomo
COLONEL THOMAS RAINBOROUGH, *a Leveller, from Cromwell's army*	Sargon Yelda
EDWARD SEXBY, *an elected representative from Cromwell's army*	Steffan Rhodri
COLONEL NATHANIEL RICH	Ash Hunter
JOHN WILDMAN, *a gentleman*	Simon Manyonda
OLIVER CROMWELL	Daniel Flynn
GENERAL IRETON	Leo Bill
GERRARD WINSTANLEY	Alan Williams
WOMAN WITH BABY	Ann Ogbomo
HER FRIEND	Amanda Lawrence
BUTCHER	Steffan Rhodri
DRUNK, *a poor man*	Alan Williams
DIGGER	Joseph Rowe

Director	Lyndsey Turner
Set Designer	Es Devlin
Costume Designer	Soutra Gilmour
Lighting Designer	Bruno Poet
Music	Helen Chadwick
Movement Director	Joseph Alford
Sound Designer	Christopher Shutt

Light Shining in Buckinghamshire was written for Joint Stock Theatre Group after a research workshop and was first performed at the Traverse Theatre, Edinburgh, in September 1976, before touring, including a run at the Royal Court Theatre Upstairs. The cast was as follows:

Janet Chappell
Linda Goddard
Bob Hamilton
Will Knightley
Colin McCormack
Nigel Terry

Director	Max Stafford-Clark
Designer	Sue Plummer
Lighting Designer	Steve Whitson
Music	Colin Sell

INTRODUCTION

You great Curmudgeons, you hang a man for stealing,
when you yourselves have stolen from your brethren all
land and creatures.

More Light Shining in Buckinghamshire,
a Digger pamphlet 1649

A revolutionary belief in the millennium went through the
Middle Ages and broke out strongly in England at the time of
the civil war. Soldiers fought the King in the belief that Christ
would come and establish heaven on earth. What was
established instead was an authoritarian parliament, the
massacre of the Irish, the development of capitalism.

For a short time when the King had been defeated anything
seemed possible, and the play shows the amazed excitement of
people taking hold of their own lives, and their gradual betrayal
as those who led them realised that freedom could not be had
without property being destroyed. At the Putney Debates
Cromwell and Ireton argued for property; Gerrard Winstanley
led Diggers to take over the common land: 'There can be no
universal liberty till this universal community be established.'
The Levellers and Diggers were crushed by the Army, and many
turned in desperation to the remaining belief in the millennium,
that Christ would come to do what they had failed in. The last
long scene of the play is a meeting of Ranters, whose ecstatic and
anarchic belief in economic and sexual freedom was the last
desperate burst of revolutionary feeling before the Restoration.

The simple 'Cavaliers and Roundheads' history taught at school
hides the complexity of the aims and conflicts of those to the
left of Parliament. We are told of a step forward to today's
democracy but not of a revolution that didn't happen; we are
told of Charles and Cromwell but not of the thousands of men
and women who tried to change their lives. Though nobody
now expects Christ to make heaven on earth, their voices are
surprisingly close to us.   —*C. C.*

Documentary Material

LIGHT SHINING
IN BUCKINGHAMSHIRE

CHARACTERS
in order of appearance

COBBE, *a gentleman*
VICAR, *an Anglican*
SERVANT
JP 1
JP 2
MARGARET BROTHERTON, *a vagrant*
STAR, *a corn merchant*
BRIGGS, *a working man*
FRIEND, *a working man*
MAN, *a vagrant*
PREACHER, *a Calvinist*
HOSKINS, *a vagrant preacher*
CLAXTON, *a working man*
CLAXTON'S WIFE
WOMAN WITH MIRROR
HER FRIEND
COLONEL THOMAS RAINBOROUGH, *a Leveller, from Cromwell's army*
EDWARD SEXBY, *an elected representative from Cromwell's army*
COLONEL NATHANIEL RICH
JOHN WILDMAN, *a gentleman*
OLIVER CROMWELL
GENERAL IRETON
WINSTANLEY
WOMAN WITH BABY
HER FRIEND
BUTCHER
DRUNK, *a poor man*

The characters Claxton and Cobbe are loosely based on Laurence Clarkson, or Claxton, and Abiezer Coppe, or Cobbe, two Ranters whose writings have survived; the others are fictional, except for those in the Putney Debates, which is a much condensed transcript of three days of debate among Army officers and soldiers' delegates which took place in 1647.

Act One

ALL (*sing Isaiah 24 xvii-xx*).

> Fear, and the pit, and the snare are upon thee,
> O inhabitant of the earth.
> And it shall come to pass that he who fleeth from
> the noise of the fear shall fall into the pit; and he
> that cometh out of the midst of the pit shall be
> taken in the snare; for the windows from on high
> are open, and the foundations of the earth do
> shake.
> The earth is utterly broken down, the earth is
> clean dissolved, the earth is moved exceedingly.
> The earth shall reel to and fro like a drunkard, and
> shall be removed like a cottage; and the
> transgression thereof shall be heavy upon it; and it
> shall fall and not rise again.

COBBE PRAYS

COBBE.

> Forgive my sins of the night and already this new
> day. Oh prevent me today from all the sins I will
> note – action, word, thought or faint motion less
> than any of these – or commit unknowing despite
> my strict guard set. Sloth not rising when Mother
> called, the air so cold, lay five minutes of sin till she
> called again. Break me, God, to welcome your cold.
> Lust when the girl gave meat last night, not keeping
> my eyes on my plate but followed her hand.
> Repented last night with groans to you, O God, and
> still dreamt. Guard me today. Let me not go to Hell,
> hot nor cold Hell, let me be one of your elect. What
> is worst, I am not praying to you about the worst
> sin. I sin in my fear of praying about that sin, I sin
> in denying my fear. But you cut through that mesh,
> knowing. Why is it not enough to use your name in
> prayer, oh God, oh Lord Jesus Christ, amen, this is

3

prayer, oh God, no swearing. Rich men of
Antichrist on horses swear, King's officers say
'dammee' laughing. The beggar swore when they
whipped him through the street and my heart leapt
at each curse, a curse for each lash. Is he damned?
Would I be? At table last night when Father said
grace I wanted to seize the table and turn it over so
the white cloth slid, silver, glass, capon, claret,
comfits overturned. I wanted to shout your name
and damn my family and myself eating so quietly
when what is going on outside our gate? Words
come out of my mouth like toads, I swear toads,
toads will sit on me in Hell. And what light on my
father, still no light? Not to honour my father is sin,
and sin to honour a greedy, cruel, hypocritical – Is it
sin to kneel here till he leave the house? I cannot go
down to him. It is sin to go down. I will wait till I
hear the door. To avoid his blessing.

THE VICAR TALKS TO HIS SERVANT (CLAXTON)

The VICAR sits at table, with wine and oranges.

VICAR.   How's the baby today? Any better?

SERVANT.   No, sir.

VICAR.   You saw who were missing again from morning
service.

SERVANT.   Sir.

VICAR.   No better – no worse, I hope?

SERVANT.   Yes, sir.

VICAR.   Good, good. The sermon would have done them
good. It wasn't my own, you could probably tell.
The Bishop's naturally more gifted. But it's no
good having it read in every parish if nobody
compels the tenants to hear it. It's the ones who
weren't there that I was talking to. 'From whence
come wars and fightings among you?' From their

lusts, from greed and envy and pride, which are from the Devil, that's where the wars come from. When you said yes, you meant no worse?

SERVANT. No sir.

VICAR. Worse.

SERVANT. Sir.

VICAR. God tries you severely in your children. It must have been a comfort this morning to have the Bishop himself encourage you to suffer. 'Be afflicted and mourn and weep.' That is the way to Heaven.

SERVANT. Sir.

He pours more wine.

VICAR. Why we have this war is because men want Heaven now. If God meant us to have heaven on earth, why did he throw us out of paradise? They're fighting God himself, do they know that? They must be brought before the magistrates and forced to come next Sunday, and I'll tell them in my own words. Thank you, a little. This is a godly estate and they will be evicted if they don't submit.

Still we must pray your baby is spared this time. Take it an orange.

He gives SERVANT *an orange.*

SERVANT. Thank you, sir.

VICAR. And if it is not spared, we must submit. We all have to suffer in this life.

He drinks.

Margaret Brotherton Is Tried

She is barely audible.

JP 1.   Is this the last?

JP 2.   One more.

JP 1.   ~~It's a long list.~~

JP 2.   Hard times.

JP 1.   Soft hearts. Yours.

JP 2.   Step forward please.

JP 1.   I still say he should have been hanged.

JP 2.   He'll die in jail. Name?

BROTHERTON. Margaret Brotherton.

JP 1.   That's no example, nobody sees it.

JP 2.   Margaret Brotherton. Begging. Guilty or not guilty?

BROTHERTON. I don't know what you mean…

JP 1.   You're not of this parish?

JP 2.   Where do you come from?

BROTHERTON. Last week I was… and before that…

JP 1.   I don't want to be told every place you've ever been. Where were you born?

BROTHERTON (*inaudible*).

JP 1.   If you belong fifty miles away what are you doing here?

JP 2.   Have you relations here? Friends you could stay with?

JP 1.   Tell us about your third cousin's wife's brother who has work for you. No? Or have you been told you get something for nothing here?

JP 2.   It's only our own poor who get help from this parish.

JP 1.	And we don't give money. So you can't drink it. It's your system of poor relief that brings them – they hear there's free bread and cheese, free fuel, there's no parish for miles that does that.
JP 2.	We can't help every vagrant in the country.
JP 1.	You must go back to where you were born.
JP 2.	If her parents didn't come from there they won't take her.
JP 1.	Her father's parish.
JP 2.	She's never been there.
JP 1.	The parish she last lived in.
JP 2.	They turned her out for begging.
JP 1.	Exactly, and so do we.
JP 2.	Why aren't you married?

BROTHERTON (*says nothing*).

JP 1.	Can we please agree on a sentence.
JP 2.	First offence. Let's be lenient.
JP 1.	It's only fair to warn you in advance that the next council meeting may reconsider the whole question of poor relief.
JP 2.	Margaret Brotherton, we find you guilty of vagrancy and sentence you to be stripped to the waist and beaten to the bounds of this parish and returned parish by parish to…
JP 1.	Where she was born.
JP 2.	To the parish where you were born. Next please.

STAR RECRUITS

A town square.

STAR.   Life is hard, brothers, and how will it get better? I
tell you, life in Babylon is hard and Babylon must
be destroyed. In Babylon you are slaves. Babylon is
the kingdom of Antichrist. The kingdom of
popery. The kingdom of the king. And it must be
destroyed. Because then will come the kingdom of
Jerusalem. And in Jerusalem you will be free. That
is why you will join as soldiers. To destroy
Antichrist. To fight with Parliament for Jerusalem.
To fight with Christ's saints for Christ's kingdom.
Because when Parliament has defeated Antichrist
then Christ will come. Christ will come in person,
God and man, and will rule over England for one
thousand years. And the saints will reign with him.
And who are the saints? You are. The poor people
of this country. When Christ came, did he come to
the rich? No. He came to the poor. He is coming
to you again. If you prepare for him by defeating
Antichrist which is the Royalists. If you join in the
army now you will be one of the saints. You will
rule with Jesus a thousand years. We have just had
another bad harvest.

BRIGGS *and* FRIEND *speak their next speeches –
indicated in square brackets – at the same time as the rest of*
STAR*'s speech from this point on.*

But, it is written, when Jesus comes 'the floors shall
be full of wheat and the vats overflow with wine.'
Why did Jesus Christ purchase the earth with his
blood? He purchased it for the saint. For you. It
will all be yours. You are poor now. You are
despised now. But the gentlemen who look down
on you will soon find out that the inhabitants of
Jerusalem are commonwealth men. Now is the
moment. It will be too late when Christ comes to
say you want to be saved. Some will be cast into
the pit, into the burning lake, into the

unquenchable fire. And some will be clothed in white linen and ride white horses and rule with King Jesus in Jerusalem shining with jasper and chrysolite. So give now, give what you can to Christ now to pay his soldiers. Christ will pay you back in diamonds. Join now for a soldier of Christ and you will march out of this town to Jersualem. Who are you? What are you? I know you all and you know me. You are nobody here. You have nothing. But the moment you join the army you will have everything. You will be as important as anybody in England. You will be Christ's Saints.

[BRIGGS.   Going for a soldier?

FRIEND.   What soldier? What side?

BRIGGS.   Parliament, inne, Mr Star?

FRIEND.   He's a gentleman, inne, Mr Star?

BRIGGS.   Parliament's gentlemen. But Parliament's for us.

FRIEND.   What's the pay?

BRIGGS.   More than I'm getting now. And they give you a musket.

FRIEND.   For yourself.

BRIGGS.   To use it. Heard about the baby.

FRIEND.   Ah.

BRIGGS.   Wife all right? Thinking of going.

FRIEND.   What about...?

BRIGGS.   Send them money. And where I am now, I'll be out again in the winter like last year. I'm not having that. You keep an eye on them. Won't be long.

FRIEND.   Christ's coming anyway.

BRIGGS.   You reckon?

FRIEND.   Something's going on.]

A LISTENER. And when will Christ come?

STAR.   When will Christ come? 'From the abomination
that maketh desolate, there shall be one thousand,
two hundred and ninety days.' Now a day is taken
for a year. And that brings us to sixteen hundred
and fifty. Yes, sixteen hundred and fifty. So we
haven't much time. Jerusalem in England in
sixteen fifty. Don't leave it too late. Join the army
today and be sure of your place in Jerusalem.

Now I've a list here of names that have joined
already. Twenty-three saints that live in this town.
Whose name is next on the list of saints?

BRIGGS.   What's the pay?

STAR.   The pay is eightpence a day. Better than labouring.
And it's every day. Not day labour. Not just the
days you fight. Every day.

BRIGGS.   And keep?

STAR.   Keep is taken out. But you're given a musket. Shall
I take your name?

Three LISTENERS *speak out.*

1.   I won't go to fight. But there's three of us could
pay for a musket among the three.

2.   I've got four silver spoons. They'd pay for
something.

3.   You can have a buckle I was given.

BRIGGS.   I'll give my name. Briggs. Thomas Briggs.

BROTHERTON MEETS THE MAN

She has several bags. He has a bottle.

BROTHERTON. Went up the road about a mile then I come back. There's a dog not tied up. So I started back where I slept last night. But that was into the wind. So I'm stopping here. It's not my shoes. I've got better shoes for walking in my bag. My sister's shoes that's dead. They wouldn't fit you. How much you got?

MAN.   Drunk it all.

BROTHERTON. I'm not asking.

He gives her the bottle.

MAN.   It doesn't matter not eating if you can drink. Doesn't matter not drinking if you can sleep. But you can't sleep in this wind.

He takes the bottle back.

BROTHERTON. What you got there?

MAN.   I thought my hands were cold but they're warm to yours.

BROTHERTON. What you got?

MAN.   Look, here, that's my Bible. That's my father's name, that's my name. Two and a half acres. I had to sell my knife. I sold my knife.

BROTHERTON. How much you got now then?

MAN.   Tenpence.

BROTHERTON. That's a long time till you got nothing. Then you can sell the Bible.

MAN.   No, I need that.

BROTHERTON. What I've got, look. The shoes. A bottle, that's a good bottle. I had another one that was no good. I don't often throw something out but I won't carry anything I don't like. A piece of cloth.

You can wrap it round. It's got lots of uses. I could
sell you that. You can't see what's in here. That's
more of my sister's things that's dead. There's a
piece of rope. You could have that for a halfpenny.

MAN.   Your face is cold. Your neck's cold. Your back's no
warmer. The wind goes right through.

BROTHERTON. You can have the rope and the cloth both for
a halfpenny.

MAN.   Come and lie down. Out of the wind. I'll give you
a halfpenny after.

BROTHERTON. No. With tenpence, we can get indoors for
that.

MAN.   Wouldn't last long.

BROTHERTON. Last more than one day. Even one day's good.

MAN.   If only I knew when Christ was coming.

BROTHERTON. You think he's coming?

MAN.   He must. If only the money would last till the world
ends then it would be all right. It's warm in Heaven.

BROTHERTON. If he comes tomorrow and you've not drunk
your money. Sitting here with tenpence in the
cold. Christ laugh at you for that.

BRIGGS JOINS UP

STAR *eats.*

STAR.   You keep your hat on. New style catching on.

BRIGGS.   Yes sir. I mean, yes, I do.

STAR.   As a sign you're as good as me?

BRIGGS.   Yes. Nothing personal, Mr Star. Before God only.

STAR.   Parson seen you like that?

BRIGGS.   He said I was a scorpion, sir. Mr Star. I mean, he
said I was a scorpion.

STAR.   A hat's all right for a soldier. It shows courage.

             Pause, while STAR *eats.*

             You know what I'm eating?

BRIGGS.   Your dinner?

STAR.   What it is.

BRIGGS.   Meat?

STAR.   The name of it.

BRIGGS.   Beef? Mutton? I can't tell from here.

STAR.   Sheep. Or, if it was, cow, but it's sheep. Now what
             language is that, beef, mutton?

BRIGGS.   It's not language –

STAR.   Beef and mutton is Norman words. The Saxon
             raised the animal. Sheep. Cow. The Norman ate
             the meat. Boeuf, mouton. Even the laws of this
             country aren't written in English.

BRIGGS.   So I've come.

STAR.   You haven't got a horse, I know, so I can't put you in
             the horse, though there's more thinking men there
             with hats on and writing their grievances down on
             paper. But you'll find plenty to talk about in the
             foot. Eightpence a day and we deduct food and
             clothing. Cheese and hard biscuit. Anything else?

BRIGGS.   You don't know how long it's going to be?

STAR.   Till we win.

BRIGGS.   That's what I mean. How long till we win?

STAR.   What we're fighting for… We've known each
             other all our lives. Our paths never cross. But you
             know me as an honest dealer. I've been leant on
             many times to keep up the price of corn when it
             could be down. And I'd be a richer man. The
             hunger now is no fault of mine. You're a Saxon.
             I'm a Saxon. Our fathers were conquered six

hundred years ago by William the Norman. His
colonels are our lords. His cavalry are our knights.
His common foot soldiers are our squires. When
you join this army you are fighting a foreign
enemy. You are fighting an invasion of your own
soil. Parliament is Saxon. The Army is Saxon.
Jesus Christ is Saxon. The Royalists are Normans
and the Normans are Antichrist. We are fighting
to be free men and own our own land. So we fight
as long as it takes. In the meantime there's no
looting. No raping. No driving off of cattle or
firing ricks. We're not antichristian Royalists.
We're Christ's saints. It's an army that values
godliness. There's no swearing. The men don't
like swearing. They like reading their Bibles. They
like singing hymns. They like talk. We don't
discourage talk. Your officers are not all
gentlemen, they're men like you.

BRIGGS.   Bacon. Is bacon Norman?

STAR.   Pork, Briggs. Pig. Very good.

BRIGGS.   And Jacob the younger brother is the Saxon herds
the pigs. And Esau the older brother is the
Norman eats the pork.

STAR.   Very good, Briggs. Excellent. Now one thing. You
wear your hat. Will you take orders?

BRIGGS.   If they're not against God.

STAR.   They can't be against God in God's army.

Hoskins Interrupts The Preacher

PREACHER. My text today is from Psalm one hundred and
forty-nine.
'Sing unto the Lord a new song and his praise in
the congregation of saints.
Let the high praises of God be in their mouth and
a two-edged sword in their hand.
To bind their kings with chains and their nobles
with fetters of iron.'

ALL AND HOSKINS. Amen, amen.

PREACHER. It is no sin to take up arms against the King. It is
no sin if we fight singing praises to God, if we
fight to bind an unjust King with chains.

ALL.   Amen.

PREACHER. For it is written: 'The saints of the most high
shall take the kingdom and possess the kingdom
forever, even forever and ever.'

HOSKINS. Forever and ever, amen.

ALL.   Amen.

PREACHER. The saints will take the kingdom. And who are
the saints?

HOSKINS. We all are.

PREACHER. The saints are those whom God has chosen from
all eternity to be his people. For he has chosen a
certain number of particular men to be his elect.
None can be added to them and none can be
taken away. And others he has chosen to be
eternally damned. As John tells us in Revelation:
'Whosoever was not written in the book of life was
cast into the lake of fire.' So it is God's saints,
chosen before their birth, written in the book of
life, who will bind the King and the nobles and
take the kingdom which will last forever.

ALL.   Amen.

HOSKINS. But no one is damned. We can all bind the King.

PREACHER. Who are the saints? They are not the same
    people who rule in this world.

HOSKINS. Amen to that.

ALL. Amen.

PREACHER. When Christ first came to earth he came to the
    poor. And it is to the poor, to you, to tailors,
    cobblers, chapmen, ploughmen, that he is coming
    again. He will not set up a kingdom like we have
    now, a kingdom of Antichrist, a kingdom of a
    king, nobles and gentry. In Christ's kingdom no
    worldly honour counts. A noble can be damned
    and a beggar saved.

ALL. Amen.

PREACHER. All that counts is whether God has chosen you.
    Look into your hearts and see whether God has
    chosen you or –

HOSKINS. He's chosen me. He's chosen everyone.

PREACHER. Or whether you are given over to the Devil. For
    those that are not saved will be cast into the pit.
    'And he that cometh out of the midst of the pit
    shall be taken in the snare.'

HOSKINS. There is no pit, there is no snare.

PREACHER. For now is the time spoken of in Isaiah, 'the
    earth is utterly broken down, the earth is clean
    dissolved.'

HOSKINS. God would not send us into the pit. Christ saves us
    from that.

PREACHER. 'And it shall come to pass in that day, that the Lord
    shall punish the host of the high ones that are on
    high, and the kings of the earth upon the earth.'

HOSKINS. Yes he will cast them down but he will not damn
    them eternally.

PREACHER. Why are you speaking? I let it pass but you are
    too loud. Women can't speak in church.

HOSKINS. God speaks in me.

PREACHER. For St Paul says, 'I suffer not a woman to teach, nor to usurp authority over the man, but to be in silence.'

HOSKINS. A text? a text is it? do you want a text?

PREACHER. 'For Adam was first formed then Eve. And Adam was not deceived but the woman being deceived was in the transgression.'

HOSKINS. Joel. Chapter two. Verse twenty-eight. 'And it shall come to pass that I will pour out my spirit upon all flesh; and your sons and your daughters shall prophesy, and your old men shall dream dreams and your young men shall see visions. And also upon the servants and upon the handmaids in those days will I pour out my spirit.'

PREACHER. It has got about that I allow answers to my sermons. But this is taking the freedom to speak too far. If anyone can call out whenever they like it will be complete confusion. I allow answers to my sermons if they are sober and godly and if the speaker has the courtesy to wait –

HOSKINS. You say most of us are damned. You say we are chosen to be damned before we are born.

PREACHER. I said to wait till the end of the sermon, and I do not allow women to speak at all since it is forbidden.

HOSKINS. How can God choose us from all eternity to be saved or damned when there's nothing we've done?

PREACHER. I will answer this question because it is a common one and others, who have the grace to wait, may be asking it within themselves. But I am not answering you. How can some people be damned before they are born? Sin is the cause of damnation, but the reason God does not choose to save some people from sin and damnation is his free will and pleasure, not our own.

ALL.   Amen.

HOSKINS. God's pleasure? that we burn? what sort of God takes pleasure in pain?

PREACHER. And those few that are saved are saved not by their own virtue though if they are the elect they will by their very nature try to live virtuously, but by God's grace and mercy –

HOSKINS. No, it's not just a few. Not just a few elect go to Heaven. He thinks most people are bad. The King thinks most people are bad. He's against the King but he's saying the same.

PREACHER. Get her out.

Two of the congregation throw HOSKINS *out.*

HOSKINS. In his kingdom of Heaven there's going to be a few in bliss and the rest of us in Hell. What's the difference from what we've got now? You are all saved. Yes, you are all saved. Not one of you is damned –

PREACHER. Woman, you are certainly damned.

CLAXTON BRINGS HOSKINS HOME

WIFE is *bathing* HOSKINS's *bruised head.*

WIFE.   What you go there for?

CLAXTON. When they beat her, you know... I couldn't...

WIFE.   But who did it?

CLAXTON. They chased her down the hill from the church and when she fell over... I couldn't stop them. I came up after.

WIFE.   But what you go there for?

CLAXTON. Just to see.

WIFE.   It's not proper church.

CLAXTON. Just to see.

WIFE.   Parson won't like it.

CLAXTON. Parson needn't.

WIFE.   I'm not going there if they beat women.

CLAXTON. No but they let you speak.

WIFE.   No but they beat her.

CLAXTON. No but men. They let men speak.

WIFE.   Did you speak?

CLAXTON. Don't want to work for parson.

WIFE.   What then?

CLAXTON. I don't know, I don't know.

    WIFE *finishes bathing* HOSKINS*'s head.*

HOSKINS. Thank you.

WIFE.   Better?

HOSKINS. Yes thank you.

WIFE.   Where you from?

HOSKINS. Near Leicester.

WIFE.   What are you doing here then?

HOSKINS. Travelling.

WIFE.   Are you married? Or are you on your own?

HOSKINS. No, I'm never on my own.

CLAXTON. Who are you with then?

HOSKINS. Different men sometimes. But it's not like you
          think. Well it is like you think. But then nothing's
          like you think. Who I'm with is Jesus Christ.

CLAXTON. How do you live?

HOSKINS. Sometimes people give me money. They give me
          for preaching. I'm not a beggar.

CLAXTON. Didn't say that.

HOSKINS. Steal though if I can. It's only the rich go to Hell.
          Did you know that?

CLAXTON. I think they do.

HOSKINS. And we don't, did you know that?

WIFE. You don't live anywhere?

HOSKINS. I'm not the only one.

WIFE. No one look after you?

HOSKINS. Jesus God.

WIFE. Are your parents living?

HOSKINS. You know how Jesus says forsake your parents. Anyone who hath forsaken houses, or brethren, or sisters, or father, or mother, or wife... or children, or lands, for my sake. See.

CLAXTON. No need to go that far.

HOSKINS. Well, it's the times. Christ will be here soon so what's it matter.

CLAXTON. Do you believe that?

HOSKINS. I do.

WIFE. But women can't preach. We bear children in pain, that's why. And they die. For our sin, Eve's sin. That's why we have pain. We're not clean. We have to obey. The man, whatever he's like. If he beat us that's why. We have blood, we're shameful, our bodies are worse than a man's. All bodies are evil but ours is worst. That's why we can't speak.

HOSKINS. Well I can.

WIFE. You haven't had children.

HOSKINS. That's all wrong what you said. We're not –

WIFE. Have you had a child?

HOSKINS. No but –

WIFE. Then you don't know. We wouldn't be punished if it wasn't for something.

HOSKINS. We're not –

WIFE.   And then they die. You don't know.

HOSKINS.   They die because how we live. My brothers did.
                    Died of hunger more than fever. My mother kept
                    boiling up the same bones.

WIFE.   Go home. Go home.

HOSKINS.   No, I'm out with God. You want to get out too.

WIFE.   No. No we don't.

CLAXTON.   Sometimes I read in Revelation. Because people say
                    now is the last days. 'And I saw a new heaven and a
                    new earth; for the first Heaven and the first earth
                    were passed away. And there was no more sea.'
                    Why no more sea? I never seen the sea. But
                    England's got a fine navy and we trade by sea and
                    go to new countries, so why no more sea? Now I
                    think this is why. I can explain this. I see into it. I
                    have something from God. The sea is water. And
                    saltwater, not like a stream or a well, you can't drink
                    it. And you can't breathe it. Because it's water. But
                    fish can breathe it. But men can't live in it.

WIFE.   What are you talking about?

CLAXTON.   What it's saying, seems to me. Fish can live in it.
                    Men can't. Now men can't live here either. How
                    we live is like the sea. We can't breathe. Our
                    squire, he's like a fish. Looks like a fish too, if you
                    saw him. And parson. Parson can breathe. He
                    swims about, waggles his tail. Bitter water and he
                    lives in it. Bailiff. Justices. Hangman. Lawyer.
                    Mayor. All the gentry. Swimming about. We can't
                    live in it. We drown. I'm a drowned man.

WIFE.   Stop it, you can't do it, you're making a fool –

HOSKINS.   No, it's good.

CLAXTON.   Octopus is a kind of fish with lots of arms grasping
                    and full of black stink. Sharks eat you. Whales,
                    you're lost inside them, they're so big, they swallow
                    you up and never notice. They live in it.

WIFE.   Stop it.

CLAXTON. We can't live. We are dead. Bitter water. There
              shall be a new heaven. And a new earth. And no
              more sea.

WIFE.   No, don't start. Don't speak. I can't.

COBBE'S VISION

ONE OF THE ACTORS (*announces a pamphlet by Abiezer Coppe*).
              A fiery flying roll: being a word from the Lord to
              all the great ones of the earth, whom this may
              concern: being the last warning piece at the
              dreadful day of judgment. For now the Lord is
              come to first, warn, second, advise and warn,
              third, charge, fourth, judge and sentence the great
              ones. As also most compassionately informing, and
              most lovingly and pathetically advising and
              warning London. And all by his most excellent
              majesty, dwelling in and shining through Auxilium
              Patris, alias Coppe. Imprinted in London, at the
              beginning of that notable day, wherein the secrets
              of all hearts are laid open.

COBBE.   All my strength, my forces, were utterly routed, my
              house I dwelt in fired, my father and mother
              forsook me, and the wife of my bosom loathed me,
              and I was utterly plagued and sunk into nothing,
              into the bowels of the still Eternity (my mother's
              womb) out of which I came naked, and whereto I
              returned again naked. And lying a while there, rapt
              up in silence, at length (the body's outward form
              being all this while awake) I heard with my outward
              ear (to my apprehension) a most terrible
              thunderclap, and after that a second. And upon the
              second, which was exceeding terrible, I saw a great
              body of light like the light of the sun, and red as
              fire, in the form (as it were) of a drum, whereupon
              with exceeding trembling and amazement on the
              flesh, and with joy unspeakable in the spirit, I

clapped my hands, and cried out, Amen, hallelujah,
hallelujah, amen. And so lay trembling sweating
and smoking (for the space of half an hour). At
length with a loud voice I (inwardly) cried out, Lord
what wilt thou do with me? My most excellent
majesty and eternal glory in me answered and said,
Fear not. I will take thee up into my everlasting
kingdom. But first you must drink a bitter cup, a
bitter cup, a bitter cup. Whereupon I was thrown
into the belly of Hell (and take what you can of it in
these expressions, though the matter is beyond
expression) I was among all the devils in Hell, even
in their most hideous crew.

And under all this terror and amazement, a tiny
spark of transcendent, unspeakable glory,
survived, and sustained itself, triumphing, exulting
and exalting itself above all the fiends. And I
heard a voice saying, 'Go to London, to London,
that great city, and tell them I am coming.'

Two Women Look In A Mirror

WOMAN 1 *comes in with a broken mirror.* WOMAN 2
is mending.

WOMAN 1. Look, look, you must come quick.

WOMAN 2. What you got there?

WOMAN 1. Look. Who's that? That's you. That's you and me.

WOMAN 2. Is that me? Where you get it?

WOMAN 1. Up the house.

WOMAN 2. What? with him away? It's all locked up.

WOMAN 1. I went in the front door.

WOMAN 2. The front door?

WOMAN 1. Nothing happened to me. You can take things –

WOMAN 2. That's his things. That's stealing. You'll be killed
for that.

WOMAN 1. No, not any more, it's all ours now, so we won't burn the corn because that's our corn now and we're not going to let the cattle out because they're ours too.

WOMAN 2. You been in his rooms?

WOMAN 1. I been upstairs. In the bedrooms.

WOMAN 2. I been in the kitchen.

WOMAN 1. I lay on the bed. White linen sheets. Three wool blankets.

WOMAN 2. Did you take one?

WOMAN 1. I didn't know what to take, there's so much.

WOMAN 2. Oh if everyone's taking something I want a blanket. But what when he comes back?

WOMAN 1. He'll never come back. We're burning his papers, that's the Norman papers that give him his lands. That's like him burnt. There's no one over us. There's pictures of him and his grandfather and his great-great – a long row of pictures and we pulled them down.

WOMAN 2. But he won't miss a blanket.

WOMAN 1. There's an even bigger mirror that we didn't break. I'll show you where. You see your whole body at once. You see yourself standing in that room. They must know what they look like all the time. And now we do.

BRIGGS RECALLS A BATTLE

BRIGGS.   The noise was very loud, the shouting and the
cannon behind us, and it was dark from the clouds
of smoke blowing over so you couldn't see more
than a few yards, so that when I hit this boy across
the face with my musket I was suddenly frightened
as he went under that he was on my own side; but
another man was on me and I hit at him and I
didn't know who I was fighting till the smoke
cleared and I saw men I knew and a tree I'd stood
under before the shooting began. But after I was
wounded, lying with my head downhill, watching
men take bodies off the field, I didn't know which
was our side and which was them, but then I saw it
didn't matter because what we were fighting was
not each other but Antichrist and even the soldiers
on the other side would be made free and be glad
when they saw the paradise we'd won, so that the
dead on both sides died for that, to free us of that
darkness and confusion we'd lived in and bring us
all into the quiet and sunlight. And even when
they moved me the pain was less than the joy.

ALL (sing from 'Song of the Open Road' by Walt Whitman).
All seems beautiful to me.
I can repeat over to men and women,
You have done such good to me,
I would do the same to you, I will recruit for
      myself and you as I go,
I will scatter myself among men and women as
      I go,
I will toss a new gladness and roughness among
      them.
Whoever denies me it shall not trouble me,
Whoever accepts me he or she shall be blessed
      and shall bless me.

THE PUTNEY DEBATES

RAINBOROUGH. The Putney Debates, October the
twenty-eighth, sixteen forty-seven. I am Colonel
Thomas Rainborough, a Leveller.

SEXBY.   Edward Sexby, private soldier, elected
representative or agitator from Fairfax's regiment
of horse.

RICH.   Colonel Nathaniel Rich.

WILDMAN. John Wildman, civilian, writer of Leveller
pamphlets who has assisted the agitators in
drawing up their proposals.

CROMWELL. Oliver Cromwell.

IRETON.   Commissary General Henry Ireton.

CROMWELL. If anyone has anything to say concerning the
public business, he has liberty to speak.

SEXBY.   Lieutenant General Cromwell, Commissary
General Ireton, we have been by providence put
upon strange things, such as the ancientist here
doth scarce remember. And yet we have found little
fruit of our endeavours. Truly our miseries and our
fellow soldiers cry out for present help. We, the
agents of the common soldiers, have drawn up an
Agreement of the People. We declare:

First: That the people of England being very
unequally distributed for the election of their
deputies in Parliament ought to be
proportioned according to the number of
inhabitants.
Second: That this present Parliament be dissolved.
Third: That the people choose a Parliament once
in two years.
Fourth: That the power of representatives of this
nation is inferior only to theirs who choose
them, and the people make the following
reservations:

First: That matters of religion are not at all
    entrusted by us to any human power.
Second: That impressing us to serve in wars is
    against our freedom.
Third: That no person be at any time
    questioned for anything said or done in
    the late wars.
These things we declare to be our native rights
and are resolved to maintain them with our
utmost possibilities.

CROMWELL. These things you have offered, they are new to
    us. This is the first time we have had a view of
    them. Truly this paper does contain very great
    alterations of the very government of the
    kingdom. If we could leap out of one condition
    into another, I suppose there would not be much
    dispute. But how do we know another company of
    men shall not put out a paper as plausible as this?
    And not only another, and another, but many of
    this kind. And what do you think the consequence
    of that would be? Would it not be confusion?
    Would it not be utter confusion? As well as the
    consequences we must consider the ways and
    means: whether the people are prepared to go
    along with it and whether the great difficulties in
    our way are likely to be overcome. But I shall
    speak to nothing but that that tends to uniting us
    in one. And I am confident you do not bring this
    paper in peremptoriness of mind, but to receive
    amendments. First there is the question what
    commitments lie upon us. We have in time of
    danger issued several declarations; we have been
    required by Parliament to declare particularly
    what we meant, and have done so in proposals
    drawn up by Commissary General Ireton. So
    before we consider this paper we must consider
    how far we are free.

WILDMAN. I was yesterday at a meeting with divers country
    gentlemen and soldiers and the agitators of the

regiments and I declared my agreement with them. They believe that if an obligation is not just, then it is an act of honesty not to keep it.

IRETON. If anyone is free to break any obligation he has entered in to, this is a principle that would take away all government. Men would think themselves not obliged by any law they thought not a good law. They would not think themselves obliged to stand by the authority of your paper. There are plausible things in the paper and things very good in it. If we were free from all other commitments I should concur with it further than I can.

RAINBOROUGH. Every honest man is bound in duty to God to decline an obligation when he sees it to be evil: he is obliged to discharge his duty to God. There are two other objections: one is division: I think we are utterly undone if we divide. Another thing is difficulties. Truly I think Parliament were very indiscreet to contest with the King if they did not consider first that they should go through difficulties; and I think there was no man that entered into this war that did not engage to go through difficulties. Truly I think let the difficulties be round about you, death before you, the sea behind you, and you are convinced the thing is just, you are bound in conscience to carry it on, and I think at the last day it can never be answered to God that you did not do it.

CROMWELL. Truly I am very glad that this gentleman is here. We shall enjoy his company longer than I thought we should have done –

RAINBOROUGH. If I should not be kicked out.

CROMWELL. – And it shall not be long enough. We are almost all soldiers. All considerations of not fearing difficulties do wonderfully please us. I do not think any man here wants courage to do that which becomes an honest man and an Englishman to do. And I do not think it was offered by anyone that though a commitment were never so unrighteous it ought to be kept. But perhaps we are upon commitments here that we cannot with honesty break.

WILDMAN. There is a principle much spreading and much to my trouble: that though a commitment appear to be unjust, yet a person must sit down and suffer under it. To me this is very dangerous and I see it spreading in the army again. The chief thing in the agreement is to secure the rights and freedoms of the people, which was declared by the army to be absolutely insisted on.

IRETON. I am far from holding that if a man have committed himself to a thing that is evil, that he is bound to perform what he hath promised. But convenants freely made must be kept. Take away that, I do not know what ground there is of anything you call any man's fight. I would know what you gentlemen account the right to anything you have in England; anything of estate, land or goods, what right you have to it. If you resort only to the law of nature, I have as much right to take hold of anything I desire as you. Therefore when I hear men speak of laying aside all commitments I tremble at the boundless and endless consequences of it.

WILDMAN. You take away the substance of the question. Our sense was that an unjust commitment is rather to be broken than kept.

IRETON. But this leads to the end of all government: if you think something is unjust you are not to obey; and if it tends to your loss it is no doubt unjust and you are to oppose it!

RAINBOROUGH. One word, here is the consideration now: do we not engage for the Parliament and for the liberties of the people of England? That which is dear to me is my freedom, it is that I would enjoy and I will enjoy it if I can.

IRETON.   These gentlemen think their own agreement is so
infallibly just and right, that anyone who doesn't
agree to it is about a thing unlawful.

RICH.   If we do not set upon the work presently we are
undone. Since the agreement is ready to our hands,
I desire that you would read it and debate it.

IRETON.   I think because it is so much insisted on we should
read the paper.

WILDMAN. Twenty-ninth of October.

IRETON.   Let us hear the first article again.

SEXBY.   That the people of England being very unequally
distributed for the election of their deputies –

IRETON.   'The people of England.' This makes me think
that the meaning is that every man that is an
inhabitant is to have an equal vote in the election.
But if it only means the people that had the
election before, I have nothing to say against it. Do
those that brought it know whether they mean all
that had a former right, or those that had no right
before are to come in?

RAINBOROUGH. All inhabitants that have not lost their
birthright should have an equal vote in elections.
For really I think that the poorest he in England
hath a life to live as the greatest he; therefore truly
sir, I think it's clear, that every man that is to live
under a government ought first by his own consent
to put himself under it.

IRETON.   I think no person hath a right to an interest in the
disposing of the affairs of this kingdom that hath
not a permanent fixed interest in this kingdom. We
talk of birthright. Men may justly have by their
birthright, by their being born in England, that we
should not seclude them out of England, that we
should not refuse to give them air and place and
ground and the freedom of the highways. That I

think is due to a man by birth. But that by a man's
being born here he shall have a share in that
power that shall dispose of the lands here, I do not
think it sufficient ground.

RAINBOROUGH. Truly sir, I am of the same opinion I was. I
do not find anything in the law of God that a lord
shall choose twenty members, and a gentleman
but two, or a poor man shall choose none. I find
no such thing in the law of nature or the law of
nations. But I do find that all Englishmen must be
subject to English law, and the foundation of the
law lies in the people. Every man in England
ought not to be exempted from the choice of those
who are to make laws for him to live under, and
for him, for aught I know, to lose his life by.

IRETON.   All the main thing that I speak for is because I
would have an eye to property. Let every man
consider that he do not go that way to take away all
property. Now I wish we may consider of what right
you will claim that all the people should have a right
to elections. Is it by right of nature? Then I think
you must deny all property too. If you say one man
hath an equal right with another to the choosing of
him that will govern him, by the same right of
nature he hath the same right in any goods he sees
– he hath a freedom to the land, to take the ground,
to till it. I would fain have any man show me their
bounds, where you will end.

RAINBOROUGH. Sir, to say that because a man pleads that
every man hath a voice, that it destroys all
property – this is to forget the law of God. That
there's property, the law of God says it, else why
hath God made that law, Thou shalt not steal? I
am a poor man, therefore I must be oppressed: if I
have no interest in the kingdom, I must suffer all
their laws be they right or wrong. Nay thus: a
gentleman lives in a country and hath three or
four lordships, as some men have (God knows how
they got them); and when a Parliament is called he

must be a Parliament man; and it may be he sees
some poor men, they live near this man, he can
crush them – I have known an invasion to turn
poor men out of doors; and I would know whether
rich men do not do this, and keep them under the
greatest tyranny that was ever thought of in the
world. And I wish you would not make the world
believe we are for anarchy.

CROMWELL. Really, sir, this is not right. No man says you
have a mind to anarchy, but that the consequence
of this rule tends to anarchy. I am confident on't,
we should not be so hot with one another.

RAINBOROUGH. I know that some particular men we debate
with believe we are for anarchy.

IRETON.   I must clear myself as to that point. I cannot allow
myself to lay the least scandal upon anyone. And I
don't know why the gentleman should take so much
offence. We speak to the paper not to persons. Now
the main answer against my objection was that
there was a divine law, Thou shalt not steal. But we
cannot prove property in a thing by divine law any
more than prove we have interest in choosing
members for Parliament by divine law. Our right of
sending members to Parliament descends from
other things and so does our right to property.

RAINBOROUGH. I would fain know what we have fought for.
For our laws and liberties? And this is the old law
of England – and that which enslaves the people
of England – that they should be bound by laws in
which they have no voice! And for my part, I look
upon the people of England so, that wherein they
have not voices in the choosing of their governors
they are not bound to obey them.

IRETON.   I did not say we should not have any enlargement
at all of those who are to be the electors. But if
you admit any man that hath breath and being, it
may come to destroy property thus: you may have

such men chosen as have no local or permanent interest. Why may not those men vote against all property? Show me what you will stop at.

RICH.   There is weight in the objection, for you have five to one in this kingdom that have no permanent interest. Some men have ten, some twenty servants. If the master and servant be equal electors, the majority may by law destroy property. But certainly there may be some other way thought of, that there may be a representative of the poor as well as the rich.

RAINBOROUGH. I think it is a fine gilded pill.

WILDMAN. Our case is that we have been under slavery. That's acknowledged by all. Our very laws were made by our conquerors. We are now engaged for our freedom. The question is: Whether any person can justly be bound by law, who doth not give his consent?

IRETON.   Yes, and I will make it clear. If a foreigner will have liberty to dwell here, he may very well be content to submit to the law of the land. If any man will receive protection from this people, he ought to be subject to those laws. If this man do think himself unsatisfied to be subject to this law, he may go into another kingdom.

WILDMAN. The gentleman here said five parts of the nation are now excluded and would then have a voice in elections. At present one part makes hewers of wood and drawers of water of the other five, so the greater part of the nation is enslaved. I do not hear any justification given but that it is the present law of the kingdom.

RAINBOROUGH. What shall become of those men that have laid themselves out for the Parliament in this present war, that have ruined themselves by fighting? They are Englishmen. They have now no voice in elections.

RICH.   All I urged was that I think it worthy consideration
           whether they should have an equal voice.
           However, I think we have been a great while upon
           this point. If we stay but three days until you
           satisfy one another the King will come and decide
           who will be hanged first.

SEXBY.   October the thirtieth.

RAINBOROUGH. If we can agree where the liberty of the
           people lies, that will do all.

IRETON.   I cannot consent so far. When I see the hand of
           God destroying king, and lords, and commons too,
           when I see God had done it, I shall, I hope,
           comfortably acquiesce in it. But before that, I
           cannot give my consent to it because it is not good.
           The law of God doth not give me property, nor the
           law of nature, but property is of human
           constitution. I have a property and this I shall enjoy.

SEXBY.   I see that though liberty was our end, there is a
           degeneration from it. We have ventured our lives
           and it was all for this: to recover our birthrights as
           Englishmen; and by the arguments urged there is
           none. There are many thousands of us soldiers
           that have ventured our lives; we have had little
           property in the kingdom, yet we have had a
           birthright. But it seems now, except a man hath a
           fixed estate in the kingdom, he hath no right in
           this kingdom. I wonder we were so much
           deceived. If we had not a right to the kingdom, we
           were mere mercenary soldiers. I shall tell you in a
           word my resolution. I am resolved to give my
           birthright to none. If this thing be denied the poor,
           that with so much pressing after they have sought,
           it will be the greatest scandal. It was said that if
           those in low condition were given their birthright
           it would be the destruction of this kingdom. I
           think the poor and meaner of this kingdom have
           been the means of preservation of this kingdom.

Their lives have not been held dear for purchasing
the good of the kingdom. And now they demand
the birthright for which they fought. They are as
free from anarchy and confusion as any, and they
have the law of God and the law of their
conscience with them. When men come to
understand these things, they will not lose that
which they have contended for.

IRETON.   I am very sorry we are come to this point, that
from reasoning one to another we should come to
express our resolutions. Now let us consider where
our difference lies. We all agree you should be
governed by elected representatives. But I think we
ought to keep to that constitution which we have
now, because there is so much justice and reason
and prudence in it. And if you merely on pretence
of your birthright pretend that this constitution
shall not stand in your way, it is the same principle
to me, say I, as if for your better satisfaction you
shall take hold of anything that another man calls
his own.

RAINBOROUGH. Sir, I see it is impossible to have liberty
without all property being taken away. If you will
say it, it must be so. But I would fain know what
the soldier hath fought for all this while.

IRETON.   I will tell you –

RAINBOROUGH. He hath fought to enslave himself, to give
power to men of riches, men of estates, to make
himself a perpetual slave. We find none must be
pressed for the army that have property. When
these gentlemen fall out among themselves, they
shall press the poor scrubs to come and kill one
another for them.

IRETON.   I will tell you what the soldier of this kingdom
hath fought for. The danger that we stood in was
that one man's will must be a law. The people have
this right, that they should not be governed but by
the representative of those that have the interest

of the kingdom. In this way liberty may be had and property not be destroyed.

RICH.   I hope it is not denied that any wise discreet man that hath preserved England is worthy of a voice in the government of it. The electorate should be amended in that sense and I think they will desire no more liberty.

CROMWELL. I confess I was most dissatisfied with that I heard Mr Sexby speak of any man here, because it did savour so much of will. But let us not spend so much time in debates. Everyone here would be willing that the representation be made better than it is. If we may but resolve on a committee, things may be done.

WILDMAN. I wonder that should be thought wilfulness in one man that is reason in another. I have not heard anything that doth satisfy me. I am not at all against a committee's meeting. But I think it is no fault in any man to refuse to sell his birthright.

SEXBY.   I am sorry that my zeal to what I apprehend is good should be so ill resented. Do you not think it were a sad and miserable condition that we have fought all this time for nothing? All here, both great and small, do think that we fought for something. Many of us fought for those ends which, we since saw, were not those which caused us to venture all in the ship with you. It had been good in you to have advertised us of it, and I believe you would have had fewer under your command to have commanded. Concerning my making rents and divisions in this way. As an individual I could lie down and be trodden there; but truly I am sent by a regiment, and if I should not speak, guilt shall lie upon me. I shall be loath to make a rent and division, but unless I see this put to a vote, I despair of an issue.

RICH.   I see you have a long dispute. I see both parties at a stand; and if we dispute here, both are lost.

CROMWELL. If you put this paper to the vote without any
qualifications it will not pass freely. If we would
have no difference when we vote on the paper, it
must be put with due qualifications. I have not
heard Commissary General Ireton answered, not
in a tittle. To bring this paper nearer a general
satisfaction and bring us all to an understanding, I
move for a committee.

End of Act One.

Interval.

Act Two

ONE OF THE ACTORS (*announces*). Information of Henry Sanders, Walton-upon-Thames, April the sixteenth, sixteen hundred and forty-nine.

> One Everard, Gerrard Winstanley, and three more, all living at Cobham, came to St George's Hill in Surrey and began to dig, and sowed the ground with parsnips and carrots and beans. By Friday last they were increased in number to twenty or thirty. They invite all to come in and help them, and promise them meat, drink and clothes.

WINSTANLEY (*announces*). The true Levellers' standard advanced, sixteen hundred and forty-nine:

> A declaration to the powers of England and to all the powers of the world, showing the cause why the common people of England have begun to dig up, manure and sow corn upon George Hill in Surrey. Take notice that England is not a free people till the poor that have no land have a free allowance to dig and labour the commons. It is the sword that brought in property and holds it up, and everyone upon recovery of the conquest ought to return into freedom again, or what benefit have the common people got by the victory over the King?

> All men have stood for freedom; and now the common enemy has gone you are all like men in a mist, seeking for freedom, and know not where it is: and those of the richer sort of you that see it are afraid to own it. For freedom is the man that will turn the world upside down, therefore no wonder he hath enemies.

True freedom lies where a man receives his nourishment and that is in the use of the earth. A man had better have no body than have no food for it. True freedom lies in the true enjoyment of the earth. True religion and undefiled is to let everyone quietly have earth to manure. There can be no universal liberty till this universal community be established.

ACTOR 1 (*announces*). A Bill of Account of the most remarkable sufferings that the Diggers have met with since they began to dig the commons for the poor on George Hill in Surrey.

ACTOR 2.   We were fetched by above a hundred people who took away our spades, and some of them we never had again, and taken to prison at Walton.

ACTOR 3.   The dragonly enemy pulled down a house we had built and cut our spades to pieces.

ACTOR 4.   One of us had his head sore wounded, and a boy beaten. Some of us were beaten by the gentlemen, the sheriff looking on, and afterwards five were taken to White Lion Prison and kept there about five weeks.

ACTOR 5.   We had all our corn spoilt, for the enemy was so mad that they tumbled the earth up and down and would suffer no corn to grow.

ACTOR 6.   Next day two soldiers and two or three men sent by the parson pulled down another house and turned an old man and his wife out of doors to lie in the field on a cold night.

ACTOR 1.   It is understood the General gave his consent that the soldiers should come to help beat off the Diggers, and it is true the soldiers came with the gentlemen and caused others to pull down our houses; but I think the soldiers were sorry to see what was done.

CLAXTON EXPLAINS

CLAXTON. Wherever I go I leave men behind surprised I no
longer agree with them. But I can't stop. Ever
since the day I walked over the hill to Wendover to
hear the new preacher for the first time. And
though I'd thought of going for weeks, the day I
went I didn't think at all, I just put on my coat and
started walking. I felt quite calm, as if nothing was
happening, as if it was an easy thing to do, not
something I'd laid awake over all night, so that I
wondered if it even mattered to me. But as I
walked I found my heart was pounding and my
breath got short going up the hill. My body knew I
was doing something amazing. I knew I was in the
midst of something, I was doing it, not standing
still worrying about it, I was simply walking over
the hill to another preacher. I'd found everything
in my life hard. But now it seemed everything
must be this simple. I felt alone. I felt certain. I felt
myself moving faster and faster, more and more
certainly towards God. And I am alone, because
my wife can't follow me. I send her money when I
can. But my body is given to other women now for
I have come to see that there is no sin but what
man thinks is sin. So we can't be free from sin till
we can commit it purely, as if it were no sin.
Sometimes I lie or steal to show myself there is no
lie or theft but in the mind, and I find it all so easy
that I am called the Captain of the Rant, and still
my heart pounds and my mouth is dry and I rush
on towards the infinite nothing that is God.

Briggs Writes A Letter

STAR.   Writing more letters? Our children grow up
             without us. Is there still no news of your wife? Do
             you think of leaving the army to look for her?
             Because if you don't go to Ireland, there's not
             much to do in the army now.

BRIGGS,   Enough.

STAR.   You make a mistake about Ireland. I understood
             two years ago, when the men didn't have their
             back pay, I was with you then. But now it's
             different. You were agitator of the regiment then
             and you still —

BRIGGS.   I still am agitator of the regiment.

STAR.   — Still think you're agitator of the regiment. I
             know that was a remarkable time for you. To be
             chosen out of so many. To stand up before the
             greatest in the country and be heard out. It's a
             council of officers now, you know that. You know
             an agitator means nothing. But you won't let it go.
             You keep on and on. The other men don't admire
             you for it.

BRIGGS.   We're demanding the council be set up like before.
             You know that. With two agitators from each
             regiment.

STAR.   I know you won't get it. Everyone knows. The
             other men laugh. You'd far better go home. Or if
             you still want to serve the cause of the saints, sign
             for Ireland. Cromwell himself is going, that says
             something. It's the same war we fought here. We'll
             be united again. We'll crush the papists just as we
             did in England. Antichrist will be exterminated.

BRIGGS.   But don't you see, the Irish —

STAR.   What, Briggs?

BRIGGS.   The Irish are fighting the same —

STAR.   The Irish are traitors. What?

BRIGGS.   Nothing.

STAR.   Show me the letter.

BRIGGS.   What?

STAR.   Show me the letter.

BRIGGS.   Can't we even write a letter now without an officer looking it over?

STAR.   It's not to your family.

BRIGGS.   No. What then?

STAR.   It's a plot.

BRIGGS.   It's a list of proposals.

STAR.   It's mutiny.

BRIGGS.   It's a list of proposals. I've made them often enough.

STAR.   You have, yes, and nobody reads them now. You draw up a third agreement of the people, and a fourth, and a tenth. It's a waste of time.

BRIGGS.   I waste a few hours then. A few days. If I don't get what I fought for, the whole seven years has been wasted. What's a few weeks.

STAR.   Show me the letter.

BRIGGS.   No.

STAR.   It wasn't an order. You have not refused to obey my order. But I won't be able to save you from mutiny if that's what you're set on.

BRIGGS.   So we can't write now. We can't speak.

STAR.   There's officers above me. Some of them think free talk doesn't go with discipline. I've always liked talk. I'd be sad to see us lose that privilege.

BRIGGS.   It's not a privilege. It's a right.

STAR.   If it's a right, Briggs, why was Arnold shot at Ware? Why were five troopers cashiered for petitioning the council of officers?

BRIGGS.	Shall I tell you why?
STAR.	It's not because I knew you before. The whole company is my friends. My rank leaves us equal before God. And yet my orders have been obeyed, because they have been seen for what they are, good orders. But lately I am talked of by my superiors –
BRIGGS.	Shall I tell you why the Levellers have been shot? Because now the officers have all the power, the army is as great a tyrant as the King was.
STAR.	I can choose to act as if no one is below me. I hope I do. But I can't pretend no one is above me. I have superior officers and I must obey. I don't think you want me removed.
BRIGGS.	You should join us against them.
STAR.	If everyone says and does what he likes, what army is it? What discipline is there? In army or government. There must be some obedience. With consent, I would say, yes, but then you must consent, or – what? If every man is his own commander? There was a time when we all wanted the same. The army was united. I gave orders from God and you all heard the same orders from God in you. We fought as one man. But now we begin to be thousands of separate men.
BRIGGS.	God is not with this army.
STAR.	It is the army of saints.
BRIGGS.	And God's saints shot Robert Lockyer for mutiny. By martial law. In time of peace. For demanding what God demanded we fight for.
STAR.	If the army splits up –
BRIGGS.	It has done.
STAR.	If you Levellers split off into conspiracies away from the main army –
BRIGGS.	It's you who've split off.

STAR.   You risk the King's party getting back again.

BRIGGS.   Would that be worse?

STAR.   Briggs. We can still be a united army. Remember
           how we marched on London, singing the fall of
           Babylon?

BRIGGS.   It's you who mutiny. Against God. Against the
           people.

STAR.   Briggs.

BRIGGS.   It's Cromwell mutinies.

STAR.   Briggs.

BRIGGS. · If I was Irish I'd be your enemy. And I am.

STAR.   Briggs.

BRIGGS.   Sir.

The War In Ireland

ONE OF THE ACTORS (*announces*). Soldier's standard to
    repair to, addressed to the army, April sixteen
    hundred and forty-nine.

Whatever they may tell you or however they may
flatter you, there's danger lies at the bottom of this
business for Ireland. Consider to what end you
should hazard your lives against the Irish: have
you not been fighting in England these seven years
for rights and liberties you are yet deluded of?
And will you go on to kill, slay and murder men,
to make your officers as absolute lords and masters
over Ireland as you have made them over
England? If you intend not this, it concerns you in
the first place to see that evil reformed here.
Sending forces into Ireland is for nothing else but
to make way by the blood of the army to
extending their territories of power and tyranny.
For the cause of the Irish natives in seeking their
just freedoms, immunities and liberties is exactly
the same with our cause here.

THE VICAR WELCOMES THE NEW LANDLORD

VICAR.   Mr Star. I wonder if I am the first to welcome you
            as the new squire.

STAR.   And the last I hope. I'm no squire.

VICAR.   You've bought the land, that's all I meant.

STAR.   I have bought the land, yes. Parliament is selling
            the confiscated land to Parliament men. That does
            not make me the squire. Just as the country is
            better run by Parliament than by the King, so
            estates will be better managed by Parliament men
            than by Royalists. You don't agree.

VICAR.   It's not for a parson to say about running an estate.

STAR.   No, but you bury the tenants when they starve.
            You'll have fewer to bury. This country can grow
            enough to feed every single person. Instead of
            importing corn we could grow enough to export it
            if all the land was efficiently made profitable. The
            price of corn will come down in a few years.
            Agricultural writers recommend growing clover on
            barren land. I will have the common ploughed
            and planted with clover.

VICAR.   An excellent idea.

STAR.   Nettles and thistles cleared, and a great crop.

VICAR.   And the little huts cleared, the squatters' huts.

STAR.   Squatters?

VICAR.   On the common. These last two years. Everyone
            hopes that now the estate is properly managed
            again they will be moved on. They are not local
            people.

STAR.   I haven't been down to the common. Well I'll
            speak to them. All over England wasteland is being
            reclaimed. Even the fens. Many years ago before
            the war, Oliver Cromwell himself led tenants in
            protest against enclosing the fens. But now he sees,

now we all see, that it is more important to provide corn for the nation than for a few tenants to fish and trap waterbirds.

VICAR. Yes indeed. Yes indeed.

STAR. When I say enclose the commons, I don't mean in the old sense, as the old squire did. I mean to grow corn. To make efficient use of the land. To bring down the price of corn. I'm sure the tenants will understand when I explain it to them.

VICAR. They will do as they're told. I'm sure you'll have no trouble collecting the arrears of rent.

STAR. I know one of the reasons they haven't paid is because they've had soldiers biletted in every cottage. So of course I'll give them time to pay. There is some talk of landlords reducing rents by as much as the tenants have paid out on the soldiers.

VICAR. I have heard talk of that.

STAR. I hope very much they're not counting on it. It would make me responsible for the keep for six years of twenty men and would beggar the estate.

VICAR. I told them that. I told them the new squire wouldn't hear of it.

STAR. In their own interests. I couldn't afford seed corn. I need two new ploughs.

VICAR. I'm sure they know their own interest. They'll pay.

STAR. I don't want to evict anyone.

VICAR. No, indeed, give them time. Three months would be ample.

STAR. I thought six.

VICAR. That's very generous. The tenants will certainly bless you.

STAR. I thought I would send for them all to drink my health and I'll drink theirs.

VICAR.   That is the custom with a new squire. It is what
          they expect.

STAR.   Is it? It's what I thought I would do.

VICAR.   Well, I can only say I welcome all the changes you
          are making. And I hope you won't make a change
          so unwelcome to the whole parish as to turn me
          away after so many years. I know the tenants here
          are as good and peace-loving as any in England,
          and I know they'll join me in supporting you in your
          plans to make this estate prosperous. It's been an
          unhappy time but the war is over. We are all glad to
          be at peace and back to normal.

STAR.   It will be hard work. For the tenants and for me. I
          don't shrink from that. It is to God's glory that this
          land will make a profit.

VICAR.   I'm sure it will.

STAR.   Don't misunderstand me, Parson. Times have
          changed.

VICAR.   I'm not against change, Mr Star. So long as there's
          no harm done.

A WOMAN LEAVES HER BABY

Two women. WOMAN 1 *is carrying a baby.*

WOMAN 1. You'll laugh.

WOMAN 2. No?

WOMAN 1. Now I'm here I can't do it.

WOMAN 2. Waiting for that.

WOMAN 1. Don't. Don't go. Don't be angry.

WOMAN 2. We come all this way.

WOMAN 1. We go back.

WOMAN 2. Why we bother?

WOMAN 1. We go back, quick, never mind.

WOMAN 2. We come so they look after her.

WOMAN 1. I can't.

WOMAN 2. I know but just put her down.

WOMAN 1. Too soon.

WOMAN 2. Put her down. Just…

> *Silence.*

> She die if you keep her.

WOMAN 1. I can't.

> *Silence.*

WOMAN 2. What you do then? You got no milk. She not even crying now, see. That's not good. You en had one, I'm telling you, she dying.

> *Silence.*

WOMAN 1. If I drunk more water. Make more milk.

WOMAN 2. Not without food. Not how ill you are.

> *Silence.*

WOMAN 1. What if nobody…?

WOMAN 2. They will. It's a special house. It's a good town. The Mayor himself. Picture inside on the wall with his chain. Mayor himself see her all right.

WOMAN 1. Another day.

WOMAN 2. She'll be dead.

WOMAN 1. If she was bigger.

WOMAN 2. You're not doing it for you. Do it for her. Wouldn't you die to have her live happy? Won't even put her down. It's for her.

WOMAN 1. Could die. Can't put her down.

WOMAN 2. Don't talk. Do it. Do it.

WOMAN 1. If she was still inside me.

A Butcher Talks To His Customers

BUTCHER. Two rabbits, madam, is two shillings, thank you.
And sir? A capon? Was yesterday's veal good? Was
it? Good. Tender was it? Juicy? Plenty of it? Fill
your belly did it? Fill your belly? It can't have
done, can it, or you wouldn't want a capon today.
Nice capon here, make a fine dinner for half a
dozen people. Giving your friends dinner tonight,
sir? And another night they give you dinner.
You're very generous and Christian to each other.
There's never a night you don't have dinner. Or do
you eat it all yourself, sir? No? You look as if you
do. You don't look hungry. You don't look as if you
need a dinner. You look less like a man needing a
dinner than anyone I've ever seen. What do you
need it for? No, tell me. To stuff yourself, that's
what for. To make fat. And shit. When it could put
a little good flesh on children's bones. It could be
the food of life. If it goes into you, it's stink and
death. So you can't have it. No, I said you can't
have it, take your money back. You're not having
meat again this week. You had your meat
yesterday. Bacon on Monday. Beef on Sunday.
Mutton chops on Saturday. There's no more meat
for you. Porridge. Bread. Turnips. No meat for you
this week. Not this year. You've had your lifetime's
meat. All of you. All of you that can buy meat.
You've had your meat. You've had their meat.
You've had their meat that can't buy any meat.
You've stolen their meat. Are you going to give it
back? Are you going to put your hand in your
pocket and give them back the price of their
meat? I said give them back their meat. You cram
yourselves with their children's meat. You cram
yourselves with their dead children.

LOCKYER'S FUNERAL

ONE OF THE ACTORS. From *The Moderate*, a Leveller
    newspaper, April the twenty-ninth, sixteen
    forty-nine.

Mr Robert Lockyer, a Leveller leader, that was
shot Friday last was this day brought through the
heart of the city. The manner of his funeral was
most remarkable, considering the person to be in
no higher quality than a private trooper. The body
was accompanied with many thousand citizens,
who seemed much dejected. The trooper's horse
was clothed all over with mourning and led by a
footman (a funeral honour equal to a chief
commander). The corpse was adorned with
bundles of rosemary stained in blood, and the
sword of the deceased with them. Most of this
great number that attended the corpse had
sea-green and black ribbons in their hat. By the
time the corpse came to the new churchyard, some
thousands of the higher sort, that said they would
not endanger themselves to be publicly seen
marching through the city, were there ready to
attend it with the same colours of sea-green and
black. Some people derided them with the name
of Levellers. Others said that King Charles had
not had half so many mourners to attend his
corpse when interred, as this trooper.

A few weeks later at Burford, the Levellers were
finally crushed.

The Meeting

A drinking place. The DRUNK *sits apart from the rest.*

HOSKINS (*to* BRIGGS). Come on, plenty to drink. Can't you
    smile? He wasn't like this last night.

BROTHERTON. What do I do?

COBBE.   Anything you like. I worship you, more than the
    Virgin Mary.

HOSKINS. She was no virgin.

CLAXTON. Christ was a bastard.

HOSKINS. Still is a bastard.

BROTHERTON. I thought you said this was a prayer meeting.

CLAXTON. This is it. This is my one flesh.

COBBE (*to the* DRUNK). Drinking by yourself? Move in with
    us, come on. Yes, we need you. Get out there when
    I tell you or I'll break your arm. That was God
    telling you.

CLAXTON. God's a great bully, I've noticed that. Do this. Do
    that. Shalt not. Drop you in the burning lake.

HOSKINS. Give us a sip. He won't give us a sip.

CLAXTON. He's not very godly. He needs praying.

HOSKINS. Let us pray. Or whatever.

    Silence.

BROTHERTON. When's he coming?

COBBE.   Who?

BROTHERTON. The preacher.

COBBE. You're the preacher.

BROTHERTON. What? No. I can't.

HOSKINS. Don't frighten her.

CLAXTON. Anyone has anything to say from God, just say it.

    Silence.

HOSKINS. There was a preacher. But his head fell off.

Silence.

CLAXTON. It's a fine shining day. Whatever troubles we have,
the sky's not touched. A clear day. Let us not lose
it. Let us remember the Levellers shot. Those at
Burford. Will Thompson and his brother. Private
Arnold shot at Ware.

HOSKINS. And the four prisoners in the tower just for
writing…

BRIGGS. Avenge Robert Lockyer.

COBBE. Lockyer's blood. Robert Lockyer's blood.
Lockyer's wounds.

BROTHERTON. I don't know these gentlemen. If they have
money. Well if you haven't and you're in the
common jail, you're lucky if you don't die. But if
they have money for the jailor he gives you a room.
With a bed and a window. I was told by a man
who'd spent all his money. If you've got money…

COBBE. Damn. Damn. Damn. Damn. Damn. There's
angels swear, angels with flowing hair, you'd think
they were men, I've seen them. They say damn the
churches, the bloody black clergy with their fat guts,
damn their white hands. Damn the hellfire
presbyterian hypocrites that call a thief a sinner, rot
them in Hell's jail. They say Christ's wounds,
wounds, wounds, wounds. Stick your fingers in.
Christ's arsehole. He had an arsehole. Christ shits
on you rich. Christ shits. Shitting pissing spewing
puking fucking Jesus Christ. Jesus fucking –

BROTHERTON. Is that from God?

COBBE. What did you say?

BROTHERTON. Is that from God?

COBBE. It is, yes. What does he say to you? Does he speak
to you? What do you answer? He'll come and
speak to you soon enough. The day he comes he'll

speak to all of us. He'll come right up to you like
this. He wants an answer. What do you say?
Nothing? He'll damn and ram you down in the
black pit. Is there nothing in you? What are you?
Nothing? (*To* BRIGGS.) Is it nothing but a lifetime
of false words, little games, devil's tricks, ways to
get by in the world and keep safe? You're plastered
over, thick shit mucky lies all over, and what's
underneath? Where's your true word? Is there
anyone left inside or are you shrivelled away to
nothing? (*To each.*) What will you say? Speak up.
What do you answer God? What do you answer?
Answer. What do you answer?

HOSKINS.   I love you.

COBBE.   There. There.

He sits down. BROTHERTON *laughs. Silence.*

CLAXTON. I tell you justice. If every judge was hanged.

HOSKINS.   I steal all I can. Rich steal from us. Everything
they got's stolen. What's it mean 'Thou shalt not
steal'? Not steal stolen goods?

COBBE.   Riches is the cause of all wickedness. From the
blood of Abel to those last Levellers shot. But God
is coming, the mighty Leveller, Christ the chief of
Levellers is at the door, and then we'll see levelling.
Not sword levelling. Not man levelling. And they
feared that. Now God is coming to level the hills
and the valleys. Christ break the mountains.

Silence. HOSKINS *holds out an apple.*

HOSKINS.   This is something held by a farmer. Then by a
stallholder. Then by me. It comes to me God's in
it. If a man could be so perfect. Look at it.

She gives it to BRIGGS, *who looks at it, then passes it
back to her. She gives it to* BROTHERTON.

BROTHERTON. I always like an apple if I can get it. I haven't
been to church for a long time. I don't know if this
is a church. It's a drinking place. I always hide on

Sunday. They notice you in the street if everyone's in church so I go in the woods on Sunday. I can't see God in this. If God was in it, he'd have us whipped.

CLAXTON. It wouldn't have you whipped, it would bless you. It does bless you. Touch it again. It blesses you. And my hand. Touch my hand. What's the matter?

BROTHERTON. Nobody touches me.

CLAXTON. Why not?

BROTHERTON. They don't touch, I don't know why, nobody touches. I don't count hitting. Nobody's touched me since…

CLAXTON. Since what?

BROTHERTON. You don't want to touch me. Don't bother. Pass it on. Pass it on.

HOSKINS. Nobody's touched you since what?

BROTHERTON. It's not right.

CLAXTON. What's not right? Touching or not touching?

BROTHERTON. Both are not right. Pass it on.

CLAXTON. They are, they're both, whichever you want, when you want, is right. Do you want me to touch your hand?

BROTHERTON. No.

CLAXTON. That's right. God's in that too. God's in us. This form that I am is the representative of the whole creation. You are the representative of the whole creation. God's in this apple. He's nowhere else but in the creation. This is where he is.

He gives it to COBBE.

COBBE.   I charge at coaches in the street. I shout at the great ones with my hat on. I proclaim the day of the Lord throughout Southwark. And what do they hear? If they could see God in this apple as I

do now, God in the bread that they will not give to
the poor who cry out day and night, Bread, bread,
bread for the Lord's sake, if they could see it they
would rush to the prisons, and they would bow to
the poor wretches that are their own flesh, and say,
'Your humble servants, we set you free.'

COBBE *gives it to the* DRUNK, *who eats it.*

HOSKINS. There's a man eats God. There's a communion.

BROTHERTON. You don't often see someone eat. They eat
when you're not looking.

BRIGGS. Friends. I have nothing from God. I'm sitting here.
Nothing. If anyone can speak to my condition.

CLAXTON. You're a soldier?

BRIGGS. I was.

COBBE. A Leveller?

BRIGGS. I was.

CLAXTON. And now?

HOSKINS. Well, a drink would be best.

CLAXTON. You'll find something. I've been different things.
When I was first a Seeker, everything shone. I
thought the third age was coming, age of the
spirit, age of the lily, everything shining, raindrops
on the hedges shining in the sun, worlds of light.
Well, we know how Parliament betrayed us. Then
how the army betrayed us. It was all a cheat.

HOSKINS. Preaching itself is a cheat.

CLAXTON. And then I saw even the Seekers were wrong.
Because while I was waiting for God, he was here
already. So God was first in the King. Then in
Parliament. Then in the army. And now he has left
all government. And shows himself naked. In us.

BRIGGS. We were the army of saints.

CLAXTON. Let it go. Move on. God moves so fast now.

HOSKINS. I try to be sad with you but I can't. King Jesus is coming in clouds of glory in a garment dyed red with blood, and the saints in white linen riding on white horses. It's for next year. Now is just a strange time between Antichrist going and Christ coming, so what do you expect in a time like this? There's been nothing like it before and there never will be again. So what's it matter now if we've no work and no food or can't get Parliament like we want? It's only till next year. Then Christ will be here in his body like a man and he'll be like a king only you can talk to him. And he's a spirit too and that's in us and it's getting stronger and stronger. And that's why you see men and women shining now, everything sparkles because God's not far above us like he used to be when preachers stood in the way, he's started some great happening and we're in it now.

CLAXTON. St Paul to Timothy, 'Let the woman learn in silence.'

HOSKINS. Jone Hoskins to St Paul, fuck off you silly old bugger.

They laugh and start getting food out. CLAXTON *holds out food.*

CLAXTON. Christ's body.

BROTHERTON. I'm afraid I haven't anything.

CLAXTON. There's plenty.

HOSKINS *holds out wine.*

HOSKINS. This is Christ's blood.

CLAXTON (*to* BROTHERTON). When did you last eat? Eat slowly now.

BRIGGS. Christ will not come. I don't believe it. Everything I've learnt these seven years. He will not come in some bloody red robe and you all put on white frocks, that will not happen. All I've learnt, how to get things done, that wasn't for nothing. I don't believe this is the last days. England will still be here in hundreds of years. And people working so hard they can't grasp how it happens and can't take hold of their own lives, like us till we had this chance, and we're losing it now, as we sit here, every minute. Jesus Christ isn't going to change it.

CLAXTON. He may not be coming in red.

BRIGGS. He's not coming at all.

CLAXTON. But in us –

BRIGGS. No, not at all.

HOSKINS. He's coming in clouds of glory and the saints –

BRIGGS. No, no, no.

COBBE. Do you think God would do all this for nothing? Think of the dead. For nothing? Why did he call me to warn London? What sort of God would he be if he didn't come now?

BRIGGS. No God at all.

CLAXTON. But in us. In us. I know there's no Heaven or Hell, not places to go, but in us. I know the Bible was written by man and most of it to trick us. I know there's no God or Devil outside what's in creation. But in us. I know we can be perfect.

BRIGGS. Then we must do it.

COBBE takes off his coat and throws it at BRIGGS's feet.

COBBE. My coat's yours. And I hope yours is mine. We'll all live together, one family, one marriage, one flesh in God. That's what we do.

HOSKINS. Yes, everything in common.

COBBE. All things common. Or the plague of God will consume whatever you have.

CLAXTON. All goods in common, yes, and our bodies in common –

BRIGGS.   No.

HOSKINS.   Yes, we'll have no property in the flesh. My wife, that's property. My husband, that's property. All men are one flesh and I can lie with any man as my husband and that's no sin because all men are one man, all my husbands one flesh.

COBBE.   I, the Lord, say once more, deliver my money which you have to cripples, thieves, whores, or I will torment you day and night, saith the Lord.

CLAXTON.   We'll take the land, all the land, and Christ will come, wait, I have something from God, Christ will come in this sense. He will come in everyone becoming perfect so the landlords all repent stealing the land. Sin is only the dark side of God. So when his light blazes everywhere, their greed will vanish – and that's how evil will go into the pit. Nobody damned, nobody lost, nobody cast out. But Antichrist cast out of us so that we become perfect Christ.

HOSKINS.   Perfect men, perfect Christ in the street, I've seen them.

CLAXTON.   The rich will be broken out of the Hell they are, however they howl to stay there, and when they're out in the light they'll be glad. They'll join us pulling down the hedges.

BRIGGS.   The landlords where they were digging at Cobham called the army in. And the soldiers stood by while the Diggers' houses were pulled down, their tools destroyed, the corn tramped so it won't grow, men beaten and dragged off to prison. The landlords gave the soldiers ten shillings for drink. Does that sound like the landlords joining us? Does that sound like heaven on earth? I've a friend wounded in Ireland and nearly mad. When they burned the church at Drogheda he heard a man inside crying out, 'God damn me, I burn, I burn.' Is that heaven on earth? Or is it hell?

BROTHERTON. It's hell, life is hell, my life is hell. I can't get
out but I'll pull them all in with me.

HOSKINS. No, wait, just wait, you'll see when Christ comes –

BRIGGS. He's never coming, damn him.

COBBE. How we know for certain that God is coming is
because of the strange work he has set us on. Who
can live through one day the way he used to? I've
seen poor men all my life. Last week I met a poor
man, the ugliest man I've ever seen, he had two
little holes where his nose should be. I said to him,
'Are you poor?' And he said, 'Yes sir, very poor.' I
began to shake and I said to him again, 'Are you
poor?' 'Yes, very poor.' And a voice spoke inside
me and said, 'It's a poor wretch, give him
twopence.' But that was the voice of the whore of
Babylon and I would not listen. And again, 'It's a
poor wretch, give him sixpence, and that's enough
for a knight to give one poor man and you a
preacher without tithes and never know when
you'll get a penny; think of your children; true love
begins at home.' So I put my hand in my pocket
and took out a shilling, and said, 'Give me
sixpence and here's a shilling for you.' He said, 'I
can't, I haven't a penny.' And I said, 'I'm sorry to
hear that. I would have given you something if
you could have changed my money.' And he said,
'God bless you.' So I was riding on when the voice
spoke in me again, so that I rode back and told
him I would leave sixpence for him in the next
town at a house I thought he might know. But
then, suddenly, the plague of God fell into my
pocket and the rust of my silver rose against me,
and I was cast into the lake of fire and brimstone.
And all the money I had, every penny, I took out
of my pocket and thrust into his hands. I hadn't
eaten all day, I had nine more miles to ride, it was
raining, the horse was lame, I was sure to need
money before the night. And I rode away full of
trembling joy, feeling the sparkles of a great glory

round me. And then God made me turn my horse's head and I saw the poor wretch staring after me, and I was made to take off my hat and bow to him seven times. And I rode back to him again and said, 'Because I am a king I have done this, but you need not tell anyone.'

HOSKINS, CLAXTON. Amen.

BRIGGS.   That man will die without his birthright. I've done all I can and it's not enough.

CLAXTON. It's not over, there's more, God hasn't finished.

BRIGGS.   I'll tell you who's with God.

He nods at the DRUNK.

BROTHERTON. No I can't. I'm not one of you, I try, you're very kind, I'm not one of you, I'm not one flesh. I'm damned, I know it.

COBBE.   You're in Hell now but you can come out. Suddenly, suddenly you are out.

BROTHERTON. I mustn't come in a place where God is. It's your fault bringing me here, I'm no good here, I can't be here –

COBBE.   We don't want any filthy plaguey holiness. We want base things. And the baseness confounds the false holiness into nothing. And then, only then, you're like a new-born child in the hands of eternity, picked up, put down, not knowing if you're clean or dirty, good or evil.

BROTHERTON. No, I'm wicked, all women are wicked, and I'm –

HOSKINS.   It's a man wrote the Bible.

CLAXTON. All damnation is, listen, all it is. Sin is not cast out but cast in, cast deep into God.

BROTHERTON. No I don't want to.

CLAXTON. As cloth is dyed in a vat to a new colour, the sin is changed in God's light into light itself.

BROTHERTON. No.

CLAXTON. That's all damnation is.

BROTHERTON. Let me go.

CLAXTON. It's only God.

BROTHERTON. I must be punished.

HOSKINS. What have you done?

BROTHERTON. Let me go.

COBBE.   No, what did you do? God is in me, asking you,
            God is asking, I am perfect Christ asking why
            you damn yourself, why you hold yourself back
            from me?

BROTHERTON. Don't touch me. I'm evil.

BRIGGS.   There's nothing you can have done.

CLAXTON. There's no sin except what you think is sin.

HOSKINS.   God makes it all, he makes us do it all, he can't
            make us sin. The men that crucified Christ, Christ
            made them do it.

BROTHERTON. The Devil, the Devil's got me.

COBBE.   A fart for the Devil.

HOSKINS.   Don't be frightened. We've got you.

CLAXTON. Sin again, do the same sin as if it were no sin –

HOSKINS.   Sin to God's glory.

CLAXTON. Then you'll be free from sin.

COBBE.   You're in Heaven, look, you're shining.

BROTHERTON. No, how can I do it again? I did it then when
            I did it. It was a sin. I knew it was. I killed my
            baby. The same day it was born. I had a bag. I put
            it in the ditch. There wasn't any noise. The bag
            moved. I never went back that way.

BRIGGS.   That's not your sin. It's one more of theirs. Damn
            them.

COBBE.   God bows to you. God worships you. Who did he come to earth for? For you. That's everyone's grief, we take it.

BROTHERTON. He wasn't baptised. He's lost. I lost him.

CLAXTON. Baptism is over.

HOSKINS. No, wait, sit down, listen –

CLAXTON. A baby doesn't need baptism, he's not born evil. He's born good, he's born God. When he died it was like a pail of water poured back in the ocean. He's lost to himself but all the water's God.

COBBE.   Believe us.

HOSKINS. He's our fellow creature, and you're our fellow creature.

CLAXTON. You're God, if you could know it yourself, you're lovely, you're perfect –

BROTHERTON. No, I'm nobody's fellow creature.

HOSKINS. God now.

COBBE.   Behold, I come quickly, saith the Lord.

CLAXTON. God's going through everything.

BRIGGS.   Christ, don't waste those seven years we fought.

CLAXTON. Everything's changing. Everything's moving.

COBBE.   And God for your sin confounds you into unspeakable glory.

HOSKINS. God has you now.

CLAXTON. Nothing we know will be the same.

BRIGGS.   Christ, help her.

CLAXTON. We won't know our own faces. We won't know the words we speak. New words –

COBBE.   Believe us.

BRIGGS.   Be safe.

HOSKINS. God has you now.

CLAXTON. Everything new, everything for the first time, everything starting –

BROTHERTON. Yes.

BRIGGS. Be safe.

BROTHERTON. Yes.

BRIGGS. So it's over.

BROTHERTON. Yes.

HOSKINS. There.

BRIGGS. You can be touched. It's not so terrible. I'll tell you what I'll do. Avenge your baby and Robert Lockyer. I'll make Cromwell set England free. And how? Easy. Kill him. Killing's no murder. He wanted to free England. That's how he'll do it. Dead.

COBBE. God won't be stopped.

DRUNK. I'm God. I'm God.

BRIGGS. Yes, amen, look who's God now.

DRUNK. I'm God. And I'm the Devil. I'm the serpent. I'm in Heaven now and I'm in Hell.

CLAXTON. Amen.

COBBE. You are God. Every poor man.

DRUNK. I'm in Hell, I'm not afraid. I seen worse things. If the Devil come at me I kick him up the arse.

CLAXTON. And that's the Devil gone.

HOSKINS. Amen, no Devil.

DRUNK. I'm in Heaven. And I go up to God. And I say, You great tosspot, I'm as good a man as you, as good a God as you.

CLAXTON. And so are we all.

DRUNK. Plenty of beer in Heaven. Angels all drunk. Devils drunk. Devils and angels all fornicating.

HOSKINS. All the light now –

COBBE.   Sparks of glory –

HOSKINS. Light shining from us –

DRUNK.   And I say to God, get down below on to earth.
Live in my cottage. Pay my rent. Look after my
children, mind, they're hungry. And don't ever
beat my wife or I'll strike you down.

BROTHERTON *gets out some food.*

BROTHERTON. I didn't give you – I kept it back – let me give
you –

CLAXTON. Yes, yes, God's here, look –

DRUNK.   And I say to God, Wait here in my house. You can
have a drink while you're waiting. But wait. Wait.
Wait till I come.

ALL (*sing Ecclesiastes 5, vii-x, xii*).
If thou seest the oppression of the poor, and
violent perverting of judgment and justice in a
province, marvel not at the matter: for he that is
higher than the highest regardeth; and there be
higher than they.
Moreover the profit of the earth is for all: the king
himself is served by the field.
He that loveth silver shan't be satisfied with silver;
nor he that loveth abundance with increase: this is
also vanity.
The sleep of the labouring man is sweet, whether
he eat little or much; but the abundance of the
rich will not suffer him to sleep.

AFTER

HOSKINS. I think what happened was, Jesus Christ did come
and nobody noticed. It was time but we somehow
missed it. I don't see how.

COBBE. It was for me, to stop me, they passed the
Blasphemy Act. I was never God in the sense they
asked me at my trial did I claim to be God. I could
have answered no quite truthfully but I threw
apples and pears round the council chamber, that
seemed a good answer. Dr Higham, I changed my
name after the Restoration.

BROTHERTON. Stole two loaves yesterday. They caught
another woman. They thought she did it, took her
away. Bastards won't catch me.

DRUNK. The day the King came back there was bread and
cheese and beer given free. I went twice. Nobody
noticed. Everyone was drunk the day the King
came back.

BRIGGS. I worked all right in a shop for a while. The
mercer had been in the army, he put up with me.
Then I started giving things away. If a boy stole, I
couldn't say anything. So when I left I thought I
must do something practical. I decided to bring
the price of corn down. A few people eat far too
much. So if a few people ate far too little that
might balance. Then there would be enough corn
and the price would come down. I gave up meat
first, then cheese and eggs. I lived on a little
porridge and vegetables, then I gave up the
porridge and stopped cooking the vegetables. It
was easier because I was living out. I ate what I
could find but not berries and nuts because so
many people want those and I do well with sorrel
leaves and dandelion. But grass. It was hard to get
my body to take grass. It got very ill. It wouldn't
give in to grass. But I forced it on. And now it will.
There's many kinds, rye grass, meadow grass,
fescue. These two years I've been able to eat grass.

Very sweet. People come to watch. They can,
I can't stop them. I'm living in a field that belongs
to a gentleman that comes sometimes, and
sometimes he brings a friend to show. He's not
unkind but I don't like to see him. I stand where
I am stock still and wait till he's gone.

CLAXTON. There's an end of outward preaching now. An end
of perfection. There may be a time. I went to the
Barbados. I sometimes hear from the world that
I have forsaken. I see it fraught with tidings of the
same clamour, strife and contention that
abounded when I left it. I give it the hearing and
that's all. My great desire is to see and say nothing.

End.

CARYL CHURCHILL

Caryl Churchill has written for the stage, television and radio. Her stage plays include *Owners* (Royal Court Theatre Upstairs, 1972); *Objections to Sex and Violence* (Royal Court, 1975); *Light Shining in Buckinghamshire* (Joint Stock on tour incl. Theatre Upstairs, 1976); *Vinegar Tom* (Monstrous Regiment on tour, incl. Half Moon and ICA, 1976); *Traps* (Theatre Upstairs , 1977); *Cloud Nine* (Joint Stock on tour incl. Royal Court, London, 1979, then Theatre de Lys, New York, 1981); *Three More Sleepless Nights* (Soho Poly and Theatre Upstairs, 1980); *Top Girls* (Royal Court London, then Public Theater, New York, 1982); *Fen* (Joint Stock on tour, incl. Almeida and Royal Court, London, then Public Theatre, New York, 1983); *Softcops* (RSC at the Pit, 1984); *A Mouthful of Birds* with David Lan (Joint Stock on tour, incl. Royal Court, 1986); *Serious Money* (Royal Court and Wyndham's, London, then Public Theater, New York, 1987); *Icecream* (Royal Court, 1989); *Mad Forest* (Central School of Speech and Drama, then Royal Court, 1990); *Lives of the Great Poisoners* with Orlando Gough and Ian Spink (Second Stride on tour, incl. Riverside Studios, London, 1991); *The Skriker* (Royal National Theatre, 1994); *Thyestes* translated from Seneca (Royal Court Theatre Upstairs, 1994); *Hotel* with Orlando Gough and Ian Spink (Second Stride on tour, incl. The Place, London, 1997); *This is a Chair* (London International Festival of Theatre at the Royal Court, 1997); *Blue Heart* (Joint Stock on tour, incl. Royal Court Theatre, 1997); *Far Away* (Royal Court Theatre Upstairs, 2000, and Albery, London, 2001, then New York Theatre Workshop, 2002); *A Number* (Royal Court Theatre Downstairs, 2002, then New York Theatre Workshop, 2004); *A Dream Play* after Strindberg (Royal National Theatre, 2005); *Drunk Enough to Say I Love You?* (Royal Court Theatre Upstairs, 2006, then Public Theater, New York, 2008); *Bliss*, translated from Olivier Choinière (Royal Court Theatre, 2008); *Seven Jewish Children – a play for Gaza* (Royal Court Theatre, 2009); *Love and Information* (Royal Court Theatre Downstairs, 2012); *Ding Dong the Wicked* (Royal Court Theatre Downstairs, 2012).

CPSIA information can be obtained
at www.ICGtesting.com
Printed in the USA
LVOW03s0301100418
572850LV00002B/2/P